The Reclamation of Self

The Reclamation of Self

HEALING THE INNER-CHILD

Michael Aiello M.S.

ISBN: 1507555407
ISBN 13: 9781507555408
Library of Congress Control Number: 2015900784
CreateSpace Independent Publishing Platform
North Charleston, South Carolina

For Nellie & Mikie
and the Inner-child within us all.

Table of Contents

Acknowledgements

❧❦

*I Acknowledge Nell Arnaud whose request that I write this book, got 'er done! Thank you, Nell, for the push. And thank you for your stewardship of the planet and loving care of me and mine. This one's for you!

*Many thanks to the Artist Conference Network which keeps me inspired, in action, and surrounded by love.

*To my daughters, Cary, Cameron, Ashley, and Tessa, who are wonderful and powerful women, and who are the symbols of my own inner-child.

*I acknowledge my great gal pals. You all walk your paths with such integrity and sass! May it always be so!

*Thanks to my Reader, darling gal pal, Terri Sternberg.

*Special mention to my beloved guides and the ever darling, Michael the Archangel.

Introduction

❦

WHEN WE NO LONGER TAKE up the whip of our negative childhood caregivers, but instead speak kindly to and about ourselves, change happens.

When we take a loving and protective stance for our inner-child, love happens.

When we release our inner-child from the encapsulated traumas within our psyches, healing happens.

When we tune-in to our inner-child daily, confidence happens.

The information and techniques in this book inspire change, love, healing, and confidence. I have been working with clients for over 25 years using these healing methods, and have witnessed these courageous people reclaim themselves in powerful and moving ways.

This is not your coverlet.
This musty rag was fashioned
From ignorance;
Crafted from criticism;
Slung down from the generations.
As I peel away this stifling thing,
The purity and pure potential
Of whom you are
Beams up through the depths.
This is your weave,
Your true and rightful bunting.

Peeling Away Negative Attachments

❦

W**HEN WE WERE LITTLE AND** we were having a wonderful time doing whatever it was we were doing, we didn't have a sense yet of social mores or an inkling that we might get into trouble; for the act we were engaged in was a pure act, bringing us joy or interest. It wasn't until the parent, or the teacher, or whomever it may have been, reacted in a negative way and threw, i.e., *shame* into the mix, that shame became attached to the action. The action first was in its purity, but now as a memory, the emotional field attached to that action is one of shame, which was embedded after the fact.

Whatever it was that we were doing as that child when we elicited shame for our action, in a different household or classroom or culture, there may *not* have been a negative response. Therefore, the action would have remained pure and there would have been no shame attached.

As negative or hostile feelings of a caregiver are attached to the actions of the child, they are introjected[1](implanted) into the psyche as a whole unit; the action coupled with the negative emotions of the parent, and the shame and conflicted feelings of the child.

As adults, we have access to this introjected coupling of action, negative emotions, and feelings of unworthiness, or badness, through memory and through triggers. (A trigger could be anyone or anything that purposefully or inadvertently makes us feel shamed or unworthy or bad). Since those negative emotions and feelings of badness are attached to our childhood actions that live within us, there is a propensity in our adulthood to believe that we were and are, indeed, bad or unworthy or unlovable. There is also a propensity to carry on the negative attitudes of the caregiver long after the fact, since those attitudes have been implanted within us. In other words, as adults, we continue to whip ourselves with criticism, ripping open the wound with yet another heart-wrenching lash.

In order to heal from these negative attachments and negative beliefs, we need to separate them out from the purity of our actions when we were children. If we sneezed into our parent's plate of food, or tripped and squashed the cake, or couldn't control our giggles in the classroom, or broke a window with a fly ball, or acted-out due to a hostile environment or feelings of unworthiness, we need to strip away the judgment and as the adult recognize that the attachments of negativity were arbitrarily placed on the action. The actions in themselves were predictable and necessary, either through innocence, instinct, playful energy, or self-preservation.

As adults, when we find we are criticizing ourselves, in self-deprecating humor, or self-admonishing remarks, we need to take action and lay the whip aside, for each lash we deliver re-traumatizes our inner-child[2]. The critical voice we employ is the introjected voice of the critical parent or caregiver, as we carry on their methodical shakedown of the child within us. Peeling away the negative attachments means to take a stand for the child within, rather than for the critical parent within. It means saying loving, not critical, things about and to ourselves. It means forgiving ourselves and the child within. It means fostering a loving environment within our psyches so our inner-child can flourish. It means reparenting our precious one.

**Exercise: Retraining your brain

Think of the negative things you say to yourself. Do you call yourself stupid or an idiot if you forget something or say something you wish you hadn't? Do you call yourself clumsy if you bump into something? Do you put yourself down in your humor? Become very conscious of what you say and think to yourself. When it is negative, say to yourself, "Stop," or "Stop it." If you are in public, it is probably best to think it rather than say it out loud, to avoid confusion and to avoid people giving you the crazy horse eye. As you continue to catch yourself beating yourself up, and continue saying, "Stop" every time, soon the brain will understand that you are asking it to do something other than play the endless loop of implanted negative judgment. The more you say, "Stop" the less you will criticize yourself until you no longer attach negative judgment to your actions. Every action has its own inherent consequence, anyway. For example, if you drop the dish on the tile it will chip or break. You don't need to pile up anymore consequences by flailing yourself. You already lost a plate; that is consequence enough. When you stop flailing yourself, you stop flailing the child within, and healing begins. When you stop flailing yourself, you take a stand for your inner-child rather than for the critical authority figure.

Gently, I lift you into my arms.
Your gangly, welted limbs
Draw into my loving embrace.
I smooth the hair out of your sweet face
Along with the tears.
I've got you now.
You are safe.

Taking A Stand

⁂

S OME HAVE HAD MORE BRUTAL childhoods than others, through beatings, abandonment, sexual abuse, cruelty, and even torture. Each bitter event is hammered into the psyche, encapsulated as a whole. When one remembers these traumas, the emotional overwhelm that was also introjected at the time is sorely felt, because one has stepped into the encapsulated moment.

These childhood traumas can leave the inner-child in a state of shock, fear, pain, rage, disassociation[3], helplessness, Post Traumatic Stress[4], shame, self-blame, powerlessness, loneliness, and low self-worth. Working though these traumas in a professional setting is an important step in healing so that one isn't ultimately left in the perilous stance of identification with the victimization of their inner-child, which leaves one stuck in that ravaged position, perceiving and creating from these shell-shocked states. Identification with the abusive figure is even more perilous, as it can cause self-loathing, vile self-criticism, self-mutilation, and/or the potential to act abusively toward others. Some go through a lifetime of being catapulted back and forth from victim to aggressor, playing out both parts in the Gestalt[5] of the traumas. Either stance holds one hostage and limits the person's ability to move out of the trauma or to move forward out of the egocentricity of the identification, for one cannot see reality holistically when one is living from the wound.

Taking a stand for the inner-child is very different from identifying oneself as the victimized child. Taking a stand for the inner-child means viewing your inner-child from the position of the adult, with love, compassion, and guidance, rather than living life as if the belt were still landing harshly, or the abandonment or neglect were taking place now. Certainly, given certain triggers, childhood traumas are reactivated throughout one's life even when one is not living from the wound. However, the difference between living from the wound vs being pulled into the wound periodically is vast.

If you find yourself ruminating about past traumas and feeling, for example, rage and indignation, or helplessness and fear, these and the other emotional states mentioned above, are vital feelings and need to be fully explored with a trusted therapist, so that you can begin to live outside of the wound and can become a loving guide for your child within. This book will help you toward that end.

**EXERCISE: FIRST CONTACT

Read this exercise first, and then close your eyes and do the exercise. Imagine a flame at the center of your heart. Imagine love in the form of light cascading from that flame, through your arms, and out through your hands. Watch the flame of light grow as it feeds itself, until it fills your entire chest cavity. Feel the waves of love.

Where do you sense your inner-child is located in your body at the moment; in your gut or in your heart or somewhere else? Place your hands on that spot and send your inner-child the waves of loving light. Flood that child! You are sending your inner-child pure love. Keep sending those waves. You may get an image of him or her, or you may not. When this feels complete, move your hands to any old scars (inner or outer) induced from childhood trauma and flood them with light. Now move to your energy system, AKA chakras, and fill all of these areas with loving light (head, neck, heart, solar plexus, belly button area, and lower pelvic area). Fill your whole body until every organ and cell is alight with love.

This exercise in itself is a powerful healing. During the day, you can send blasts of loving light to your inner-child, especially after upsetting situations. Do this exercise as often as possible.

* If you are having trouble with this exercise, keep at it, and the love will grow. And don't worry, you will be making contact in other ways and bringing love in many forms to you inner-child in the up-coming chapters.

Here My Precious One.
A nest for you made of light.
Bend the filaments this way, and a
Meadow appears:
Lazy butterflies, soft humming sounds,
a drowsy Sun.
Bend the filaments that way, and frothy
Turquoise waves
Crescendo in wild symphony, and in the
Distance, sea caves beckon with glittery
Treasure.
As we dance with the light, the Black
Stallion tosses his silky head and keeps
A watchful eye; and so do I My Sweet,
And so do I.

Creating A Safe Place

❧❧

W HAT WOULD A SAFE PLACE look like to you and to your inner-child? If you could take a magic wand and create the perfect place, what would it look like? Where would it be? Would it be in the woods, in a meadow, near the ocean, in an oasis in the desert, in a cottage, in a fortress, or on another planet? What would the terrain look like? Would you have animals present, real or mythical? This safe place will reside within you, in your psyche, where you can go in your imagination and where your inner-child can go and feel safe and protected and happy. Where would he or she like to hang out? Would there be unicorns, dolphins, horses, books, art supplies, bucket and shovel, or hidden treasure? You get to create it exactly as you want it, every beautiful detail; every leaf, every smell, every bird call, if you choose to have birds present. Are you already getting a sense of it?

Now, close your eyes and take that magic wand and take all the time you need to create your perfect safe place.

Can you imagine your inner-child hanging out here? If you handed the magic wand to your inner-child, what would s/he add?

Take a stroll through the beautiful place you just created. How does it feel? How do you feel? What is the temperature like? Is there a breeze? Are you inside or outside? Take a deep breath and take it all in. This is your place, made especially for you and your inner-child by you and your inner-child.

**Exercise: Welcoming your inner-child

If your inner-child has not already popped into the newly created safe place, now is the time to put out the welcome mat for her/him. Your inner-child is you when you were young; the age depends upon the memory or circumstance. Invite your inner-child into the safe place. Who shows up? Do you get a sense of your inner-child? About what age is s/he? Does your inner-child have a sense of you? Does our inner-child know who you are? Are you embracing? Take your time explaining the situation; explain to your inner-child that you are his/her future-self, that s/he is always with you and is never alone; that you have created this special place for him/her and that you will visit often. Are you able to tell your inner-child how much you love her/him? Take your time.

If you feel you are not yet ready to be present with your inner-child, you can invite your inner-child into the safe place while you keep the imaginal distance in your easy chair, or couch, or wherever you are as you create the safe place. The most important things right now are that your inner-child has a safe place in your psyche and that when you are present with your inner-child you come as a loving guide.

My sword catches the glint of the sun
As I lay another poison dart to rest.
Come my Little One,
Let's seek out the company of
The gentle folk.

Stepping Into The Cougar

❧

PROTECTING AND TAKING A STAND for the inner-child means not only laying aside the lash of self-criticism, negative self-talk, self-deprecating humor, etc., but also of aligning with relationships whereby the inner-child thrives rather than is re-traumatized. As we are at times held captive by the introjects of our childhood, so our inner-child is held captive by *our* actions *now*. Since the inner-child lives within *us,* it is up to us to protect our inner-child. There are varying degrees of negative and wounding relationships; some are physically and/or sexually abusive, some emotionally abusive, and some more subtle, with stinging barbs that leave the inner-child confused, hurt, and stripped of power. These relationships could occur with a spouse, partner, family member, friend, etc. Some relationships are more important than others, and so are worth resolution through dialogue and/or counseling. Shifting the dynamics of a painful relationship, or stepping away from a relationship that continues to pierce, releases the inner-child from further abuse.

When we step into our cougar, we step into whatever force that is within us that draws the line in the sand and says, "No More. No more messing with me! No more digs, no more manipulation, no more lies, no more power thievery." What is that force within us that brings us to that point where we no longer stand within the range of a poisonous dart? What is that within us that brings us to the seat of our power?

Many keep these relationships that are abusive in one way or another. Is it because of loneliness or the fear of being alone? And yet, there is a precious relationship waiting for us at the center of our core. If we consciously reach out, and daily tune-in to our inner-child, the recognition that *we* are not alone, is palpable. It is a two-way street; when we tune into our inner-child and develop the relationship, our inner-child gets it that they are not alone and they are not so frightened. And as we develop the relationship with the inner-child, *we* get it, the adult *us* gets it that *we* are never alone. We have this bright star-child reaching out for us who is lives within us, who is never going to go away. This inner-child is the pure essence of who we are; the pure potential of us. This is the great relationship with the Self. Not the shallow, ego relationship, of "what do people think of me, how do I look, or how much money am I making," but the vital relationship of coming back to the Self. The reclamation of the Self is the relationship with the inner-child. It is fostered with our integrity, our self-care, standing by our word, not letting anyone push us around, not pushing anyone else around, not caring if people don't get it, not caring about judgment, and in knowing who we are and knowing that we have found ourselves.

****Exercise: Being the Cougar**

Think of the cougar; its strength, its power, its beauty, the soft fur, the golden glint, the gentle chuff it makes when content. Now think of the cougar as someone comes along with a stick and tries to give it a whack. How does the cougar react? The cougar will have none of it for sure. Either it retreats and forever steers clear of the person, or the cougar reacts in such a way that the person would never take up that stick again. Either way, walking away from a poisonous dart or clearly stating that you will have none of it, is both protective and powerful, for it is a stance that says, "No more!"

Now think of any relationships in your life that leave you feeling powerless, pierced, confused, or belittled. As the cougar, do you need to distance yourself from the relationship or confront the poisonous dart directed at your heart? Or both?

Tips for confrontation:

*Ask the person if they meant to pierce you. Sometimes people aren't aware of the tender wounds in one's psyche and don't realize they have just stepped on a land-mine. This gives the person the benefit of the doubt, and alerts them that there are sensitive areas to keep in mind.

If the person did mean to pierce, just asking the question brings it out in the open and they are less likely to throw another dart and get 'caught out again.'

*If someone continues to pierce after you have dialogued with them, and you feel you have been clear, then ask yourself if it is time for more dialogue, or time to move it to a third party (counseling), or time to distance yourself from the relationship. What does the cougar say?

*If you are being physically or mentally abused, seek counseling immediately. If it is not safe to do so or you are in danger, call the Domestic Violence Hot Line and they will get you (and your children) to safety. The Domestic Violence Crisis Centers can help with counseling as well as with legal help.

I step into the encapsulated moment,
Fierce and loving.
You leap into my arms and we twirl in
A fusion of love.
Hand in hand we step out of time, into
A nest of light while I whisper sweet
Everythings.
As I look back over my shoulder, your
Assailant turns into a pillar of salt;
Dread words lay granulated and lifeless
In the dust, along with fell intentions.
I tell you what you need to know:
It was never your fault.
I am always with you.
You are precious.

Stepping In And Out Of Time

❧

YOUR PAST IS NOT LAID out behind you, *out there* somewhere, but rather, carried within you, alive in your psyche. If you were traumatized as a child, that trauma was encapsulated within your psyche, along with the emotional overwhelm you experienced at that time. If you were four years old, for instance, at the time of this particular trauma, the encapsulated emotions will be that of a four year old. If you had no protector during the trauma, then as an adult, anytime you feel threatened, you may well find yourself catapulting through time and space to become that undefended child yet again. You may be flooded with fear, confusion, paralysis, and an inability to articulate as you enter the emotional field of the encapsulated trauma.

In this way, you have direct access to your inner-child, however unintended it may be. You can feel the potency of the emotions, the aliveness of the past, and the helplessness of the four-year-old you. It is usually later, well after the threat has passed, when you have 'recovered yourself,' that you have the ability to assess the situation through the eyes and the emotional field of the adult you.

Have you ever noticed that when you think or talk about past traumas, you find yourself dragged down into the rawness of the emotional overwhelm? Your intention may have been only to allude to the trauma, but did you find that the more you thought about it or the more you talked about it, the more it gripped you? When we think about or talk about a trauma that has happened to us in the past, we not only step into the memory of ourselves as a child, we step into the encapsulated moment of the trauma, which is alive, laden with heavy emotions and raw wounds, and where we find our inner-child still swimming in the sea of the trauma.

With intention, we can step into the memory of the trauma, and rather than seeing from the perspective of the child, we can visit as the adult; as the future-self of our inner-child. As the loving adult, we can step into the memory in the position of the Observer, and have access to our inner-child in the encapsulated trauma. As the loving guide, we can escort our inner-child out of the moment before the trauma takes place once again, and guide them to the safe place we have created in our psyches, leaving the angry or inappropriate parent or caregiver behind, ineffectual, with nobody there to traumatize.

We can do this with every memory that carries within it a wound, whether slight or great. On the way to the Safe Place, we need to let our inner-child know that the fault isn't theirs; that they are never alone; that they are loved and precious. As you can imagine, the healing is profound each time we do this. And as we do this, the more the memories will surface as the psyche stretches towards wholeness and healing, like the tender sapling toward the light.

****EXERCISE: STEPPING IN AND OUT OF TIME**

Allow your unconscious mind to select a childhood memory that carries within it a wound. As the future-self of your inner-child you are about to step into this memory as the Observer. Look now into the memory and see what is about to take place. You are standing just on the outside of the encapsulated trauma, looking in. Your inner-child is within the encapsulation along with whomever is about to inflict the wounding. Step in now. Hold your hand up to silence or stop any negativity that is about to happen. Freeze the figure who carries the negative intention, and turn your attention to your inner-child. Gather your inner-child into loving arms. Let them know you are their future self. Tell them what they need to know: they are not at fault, they are never alone, they are precious.

Let your inner-child know that you are going to escort them out of the trauma, into a wonderful place that is safe and where s/he is free to play, heal, and grow with love. Take her/him there now. Show your inner-child around. Let your inner-child know you will visit there often. Say all of the things s/he needs to hear. What does s/he need to tell you? Gather him/her into your arms once more and say your good-byes.

(If you have been sexually abused or severely physically abused or suspect sexual abuse that hasn't surfaced yet, do this exercise with your therapist so that s/he can guide you through this process).

Angel of Mercy
Hear our prayer.

Angel Of Mercy

❧❧

MANY YOUNG PEOPLE HAVE SUFFERED tragically harsh lessons in life through their naiveté, alcohol or drug-induced states, peer pressure, egocentrism, rage, a momentary lapse of attention, ignorance, desperation, and/or denial of their own or their peers' mortality.

Too many teens and young people in their twenties have been the cause of fatalities and serious injuries while driving in an altered state of consciousness; so many beautiful teens coming home from prom or graduation with shattered lives, or not coming home at all.

Too many college students have died on their 21st birthday trying to drink 21 shots between the hours of midnight and when the bars close, which gives them, with the help of their peers, one to two hours to consume those 21 shots; the 'helpful' peers being filmed pouring shots down the throat of the already staggering, falling, incoherent birthday boy or girl. So many promising youth awakening the next morning to tragedy, or not awakening.

Too many dares, too much exclusion, too many bullies, too much testosterone, too many risks, too young, too unknowing; whatever the cause of the loss and the shattering, it's too tragic, too much for anyone to bear.

And yet, how many of our youth carry the burden of tragic loss and crippling guilt, their lives shattered from carelessness, a wild party, or a miscalculation? As these youth grow into adults, piecing their lives back together, they carry within them the inner-child who relives over and over the tragedy, suffering the loss, the shock, and the hideous guilt again and again.

And who can release the inner-child from this nightmare? Loving and forgiving family members and friends offer tremendous solace, thank God for them, if one is lucky enough to have that; forgiveness from the family where the tragedy struck is heaven sent, if it comes; a wonderful therapist would be a prayer answered; and a healing through the divine hand, blessed. And yet, it is The Angel of Mercy who must finally step in to release the inner-child from this living hell.

And if it is you, who carries within your psyche, this inner-child, then you are that Angel of Mercy. It is you who have the ability to go into the encapsulated moment where the tragedy is playing itself out. It is you, as the loving guide and forgiving angel, who can tell your inner-child what they need to hear; you who can escort them to the safe-place within your psyche; you who can love them unconditionally; and it is you who holds the power to forgive, and therefore, to release.

**EXERCISE: FORGIVENESS

Waves of guilt alert one that their inner-child needs tender mercy. The inner-child could be any age: very young, a teen, in the early twenties, older, and still older, yet. Whoever we are today, we are wiser than a few decades ago, a few years ago, a few months ago, and even wiser than yesterday. And so in essence, as the wise and loving guide with vast experience from life's lessons, we have the ability to forgive the younger versions of ourselves and release those younger versions from the burden they carry.

As in Stepping in and Out of Time, step into the memory of the trauma as the Observer; the loving adult. Guide your younger-self to the safe place in your psyche. As the Angel of Mercy, fold them gently into your arms and tell them what they need to hear; how you love and forgive them; how you intend from this minute forward to treat yourself tenderly as well as those around you. Do this exercise as often as you need to. There will be layers to the guilt and to the release.

You took the hand that led.
Of course you did.
You were just a child.

Betrayal

✣✣

FOR SOME CHILDREN, THE FEAR of monsters lurking in the dark closet or coiled under the bed was not an unrealistic fear. For them, the monster may have turned out to be a parent, an older sibling, a grand-parent, a close family friend, or the babysitter, scout leader, priest, teacher, etc.; the list sadly goes on. For some, there is more than one monster, for once the little hand has trusted the lead, that child is more susceptible to betrayal by others.

Molest is a devastating misuse of love, power, trust, and guidance. It is a physical and emotional abuse that carries with it the potential to rip and tear the body, mind and psyche of the child. The juxtaposition of betrayal, shock, terror, pain, threats, denial, secrecy, or lies, with that of the child possibly being told that they are special, beloved, desirable, etc., along with the possibility of experiencing feelings of pleasure, creates a psychic bomb that is too huge for the child to contain. The betrayal, alone, is too great for the child, and so the child will dissociate rather than shatter, by leaving the body during the abuse and eventually go into denial that any abuse ever took place, until memories are allowed to surface when they are older and able to contain the terrible scope of the betrayal.

The guilty party is that of the betrayer, of course, not the child, even if the child felt desire, pride, or pleasure; for the hand that led them, took them to a place where these things readily exist. The onus lay with the guide, not the trusting child. The cloak of shame belongs to the one who broke the trust, not the child who was duped or was seeking love and approval.

The guilty party is also not the child who may have acted out the sexual abuse when older, either through promiscuity, rage, depression, sexual repression, fear, poor grades, perfectionism, control issues, etc., in order for the deep wounds of the psyche to release some of its burden.

The guilty party is also not the child that the abuser cultivated as the family scape-goat. What better way to make sure no one would believe any story the child might leak? The answer is to simply make that child into a liar, a black sheep, a leper.

And so, what does this beautiful, fragile inner-child need? S/he needs your unconditional love, empathy, and forgiveness. Remove that cloak of shame or blame, for the fault lies not with you as that child, nor with you as the acting-out teen. The betrayal caused a deep psychic wound that has been playing itself out, as psychic wounds do. It was never your fault. You are not to blame.

**EXERCISE: RELEASE

If you haven't already sought out therapy around the issue of molest, now is the time to do so. A therapist can create a safe container for you to begin the healing process. With your therapist, or if you have already received therapy, go into the memories where your inner-child is carrying shame, blame, guilt, feelings of unworthiness, or self-loathing, and as the loving adult, let your inner-child know s/he is not to blame and let her/him know how precious s/he is. These memories may span over several years, and so your inner-child will need your tender mercy and guidance many times over.

The grace descends
Upon us
As
Three are healed
In
One.

Three Are Healed In One

❧

As WE CARRY FORTH THE battle-scars of our youth, we also carry within us the negative patterning of those who inflicted the wounds. And so when we have children of our own those old reels that were stored deep within the psyche can jump to life, over-riding even our most positive intentions as a parent.

It works like this: If you were yelled at or shamed or hurt by a caregiver, those scenes were introjected (implanted) and stored in your psyche like a two-reeled film clip. The more times the negative behaviors were inflicted upon you, the more substantial the reel, or patterning. The one reel is you receiving the verbal or physical punishment and the other reel is your parent doling out that punishment. When you have children who reach the age that you were when you got into trouble, the possibility is great that if they do the very thing that got you into trouble, it will trigger the dormant reels into action. If all of a sudden you feel an uncalled for rage, you have just been taken hostage by the introject of your parent and have become the unwitting projector. The stored scenes jump to life and your child becomes the backdrop of the first reel, and the symbol or stand-in for your inner-child. Dread words may begin to fly out of your mouth;

the very ones you swore you would never utter, as the stored memory and the stored emotional state of your parent, speak through you.

If, at this time, you step into the position of the Observer rather than the Projective[6] position, and realize that you are playing out an old negative dynamic, the healing potential is great for you, your child, and for your inner-child. When you learn to over-ride the patterning, and whenever you parent the way you wished you had been parented, you can feel the grace descend upon you and your child and your inner-child as three are healed in one.

**EXERCISE: CREATING NEW POSITIVE PATTERNING

Understanding the basics of introjection and projection, is the first step in unraveling or re-patterning the inner-reels. The second step requires setting the stage in advance. Now that you understand that your child's behavior can trigger the stored psychic reels into action, you will need to rehearse in your mind many times what you will do the next time your child exhibits that particular behavior. By doing this you are creating etchings of a new pattern and an alternate route to take when the dormant reels come to life. Remember, the old pattern has deep grooves and jumps to life with a charged emotional field. Since the charged emotional field is the glue that holds the reel together, you will be standing in the center of an emotional lake when your child inadvertently triggers the reels into action.

When feeling triggered, the best thing to do if possible, is to leave the room immediately before any words or gestures can escape, and simply feel the magnitude of the emotional take-over from the position of the Observer. Stand for a few minutes until you feel the emotional charge dissipate. By doing so, you have just shifted the patterning in two ways:

1) You left the scene without allowing the introject to speak through you.
2) You felt the emotional field from the Observer view point rather than from the Projective one. In other words you observed the huge emotion racking you without directing it at your child. Once you realize the dynamic is within you and it is not really about your child, the shift in the patterning is already taking place. You have just created new patterning etchings that overlay the old deep grooves. When you go back to your child, you can speak from your positive intentions rather than from the old negative patterning. The more times you are successful, the deeper the new grooves, until you won't need to go in the other room any longer.

The deeper the new positive patterning, the more you unravel the old negatively charged one. As you speak tenderly to your child, your inner-child also reaps the benefits, and therefore you, as well, as three are healed in one.

Soft sonar blips rise
From the murky depths.
Let my love light the way.

Tuning-In

✢✢

OUR INNER-CHILDREN CERTAINLY LET US know when they are in distress as they send up waves of fear, shame, paralysis, etc. If you can locate where in the body the alarm is coming from, and you place your hand over that spot and send calming waves of love and reassurance, you will have accomplished a few things:

* You have let your inner-child know they are not alone.
* You have let your inner-child know they are loved and protected.
* You have held on to your adult stance rather than being catapulted back in time as the child.
* You have opened up the possibility for a new response to a situation which triggered the distress.

Truly, if you can't locate where the alarm is coming from, the mental tune-in alone accomplishes the same thing. However, if you can locate that area in your body, your warm hand and focused energy is like a laser beam to your inner-child. If you are in a situation where people are around, they will have no idea why your hand is on your stomach or heart or elsewhere, and they will have no idea that you are communing with your inner-child. But your inner-child will know. And as your inner-child calms, you will be able to address the situation in a new manner.

You can use this method *before* your inner-child sends distress signals when you know what kind of situations trigger past trauma or when the thought of new situations, such as public speaking or job interviews cause fear or anxiety to cascade through your system. When you reassure your inner-child before the fact, and tell them that you will handle the situation and that they can go hang out in their Safe Place, you will begin to enter situations with much more confidence and calm. How great is that?

If you are having trouble imagining or tuning-in to your inner-child, you can pick out a stuffed animal or a baby doll that you resonate with and call it by your childhood name. You can hold, rock, and pat your inner-child stand-in, and tell her/him all the things they need to know. Be ever so gentle with this stand-in; this is not a toy, for this is the symbol of your inner-self. If you have trouble sleeping or have nightmares, you can tell this stand-in just before sleep, that they are safe and that you are with them always and will always keep them safe.

**EXERCISE: DAILY TUNE-INS

* Locate in your body where you feel your inner-child is located and send waves of love and healing light.
* Send reassurance to your inner-child before any upcoming stressful situations.
* Tell your inner-child daily that they are never alone and that you are always with them.

- Tell your inner-child daily that they are precious.
- Tell your inner-child daily that they were never at fault.
- If your inner-child sends up an alarm, place your hand over that part of your body where you feel the most intense emotion, and send reassurance to your inner-child that s/he is safe and protected.

When you tune-in to your inner-child daily, your inner-child won't feel so isolated or frightened and the healing process is well on its way.

Things To Remember

❦

- Say only positive things to and about yourself daily.
- Be ever so gentle with yourself.
- Don't allow anyone to abuse you in any way, including yourself.
- Take a Stand for your inner-child.
- Step in and out of time, and guide your inner-child to safety.
- Create a safe place in your psyche for your inner-child.
- Place your hand on your body where you feel your inner-child is located, and send waves of love.
- Parent your children with the healing of your inner-child in mind.
- Calm your inner-child when you are in distress or feeling anxious.
- Your inner-child needs your love, forgiveness, and tender guidance.
- As you re-parent your inner-child, your inner-child will begin to thrive and then of course, so will you.
- A trusted therapist is a wonderful resource in helping you on your healing path.

Good luck and may God speed you on this incredible healing journey that you so deserve.

**EXERCISE: LOVE NOTES

Write ten love notes to your inner-child. For example, Dear (childhood name), You are so precious to me. I love you, (Adult name). Or, Dear_____, It was never your fault. I love you, _____. Write ten of these gems and hide them around the house. Put one in the frig, one in a sock drawer, etc., and as you discover them, and your inner-child gets to read them, re-hide them in different locations. These notes are a direct blast to your inner-child from their beloved you.

ENDNOTES:

A LOOK AT SOME PSYCHOLOGICAL CONCEPTS

1. **Introjection:** An unconscious process by which an external object is symbolically taken in and assimilated as part of oneself (Sandler, cited in Gabbard, 1994, p.49). I use this term not only to signify the taking in of the object (negative caregiver, trauma, abuse) but the emotions, as well, that were felt by the child and, incredibly, that were felt by the negative caregiver. I see the whole event being introjected into the psyche of the child.

2. **Inner-child:** Alice Miller (1991, p.3), speaks of the inner-child as "the neglected child we once were, the child that was once abandoned and betrayed. It waits for us to summon the courage to hear its voice. It wants to be protected and understood, and it wants us to free it from its isolation, loneliness, and speechlessness."

3. **Dissociation:** Jung (cited in Samuels, Shorter, & Plaut, 1986, p.47) referred to dissociation at the "unconscious fragmenting of what should be linked in the personality, a kind of 'disunion with oneself'." Freud (cited in Jacobi, 1962, p. 56) saw dissociation as a displacement of energy, where "energy lost by consciousness passes into the unconscious and activates its contents -- archetypes, repressions, complexes, etc. -- which embark on a life of their own and irrupt into consciousness, often provoking disturbances...."

I have had many clients describe to me how they floated up and out of their bodies during abusive situations, especially sexual abuse. Dissociation protects the child from experiencing the full impact of the abuse as well as from tormenting memories. Hilgard (cited in Hawthorne, 1983, p.3) suggests that the dissociated systems are relatively coherent patterns of behavior with sufficient complexity to suggest some degree of internal organization, Usually an amnesic barrier prevents integration of the dissociated systems, at least during the time that the dissociation persists. Alice Miller states that every abused child "must totally repress the mistreatment, confusion, an neglect it suffered. If it were not to do so, it would die. The child's organism could not withstand the dimensions of this pain" (1991, p. 82).

4. **Post Traumatic Stress Disorder (PTSD):** According to Heidi Vanderbilt (Lear's, 1992), PTSD is prevalent among incest victims. The victims had the same PTSD symptoms as did some Vietnam War veterans and most victims of torture. The symptoms include, but are not limited to, amnesia, nightmares, and flashbacks. "People who have PTSD may 'leave their bodies' during the abuse, and they may continue to dissociate for decades after the abuse ends." The nightmares of the incest victims "involved being chased, and stabbed, suffocated, made immobile and voiceless."

5. **Gestalt:** A Psychological Therapy developed by Fritz Perls. One of the key concepts of his therapy is that "nothing exists except the 'now'" (Corey, 1991, p. 233). I use this term as an adjective to illustrate how memory or triggers or patterning

launches us into the immediacy of the moment where the abuse is playing out.

6. **Projection:** "Projection is the reverse of Introjection. In projection, we disown certain aspects of ourselves by assigning them to the environment. When we are projecting, we have trouble distinguishing between the inside world and the outside world. Those attributes of our personality that are inconsistent with our self-image are disowned and put onto other people" (Corey, 1991, p. 237).

REFERENCES

Corey, G. (1991). <u>Theory and practice of counseling and psychotherapy</u>. Brooks/Cole Publishing Co.

Gabbard, G. (1994). <u>Psychodynamic psychiatry in clinical practice</u>. American Psychiatric Press, Inc.

Hawthorn, J. (1983). <u>Multiple personality and the disintegration of literary character</u>. New York: St. Martin's Press, Inc.

Jocobi, J. (1962). <u>The psychology of C.G. Jung</u>. Yale University Press.

Miller, A. (1991). <u>Breaking down the wall of silence</u>. Penguin Books, USA, Inc.

Samuels, A., Shorter, B., & Plaut, F. (1986). <u>A critical dictionary of Jungian analysis</u>. Routledge.

Vanderbilt, H. (1992, Feb.). Incest - a chilling report. <u>Lear's</u>.

www.ingramcontent.com/pod-product-compliance
Lightning Source LLC
Chambersburg PA
CBHW030522290526
45786CB00004B/1570